Dear Parent,

Learning the alphabet is an important first step on the road to reading. *Alphabet Puzzles and Games* will help your child identify letters and sounds. The book includes mazes, hidden pictures, puzzles, dot-to-dots, and lots of practice working with letters. To get the most from *Alphabet Puzzles and Games*, follow these simple steps:

- Find a comfortable place where you and your child can work quietly together.
- Encourage your child to go at his or her own pace.
- Help your child sound out the letters and identify the pictures.
- Offer lots of praise and support.
- Let your child reward his or her work with the included stickers.
- Most of all, remember that learning should be fun! Take time to color the pictures, laugh at the funny characters, and enjoy this special time spent together.

Amy and the Apples

Help Amy get to the basket of apples.
Follow the path that shows **A** or **a**.

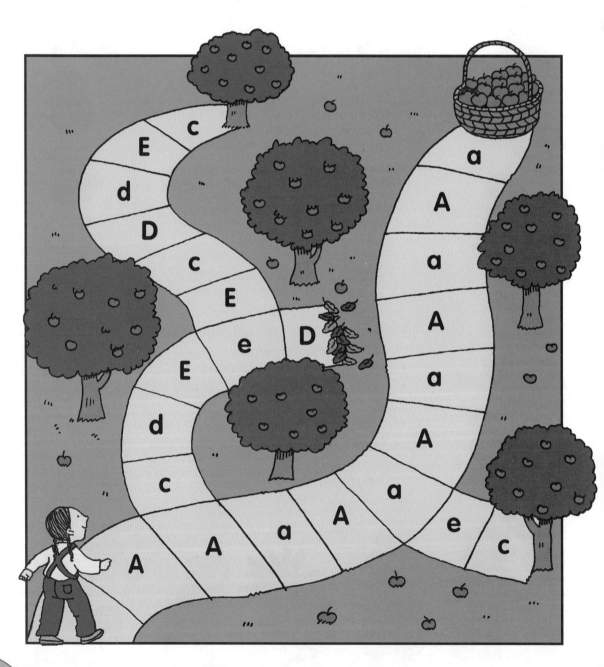

In the Air

Color the spaces that show **A** or **a**.

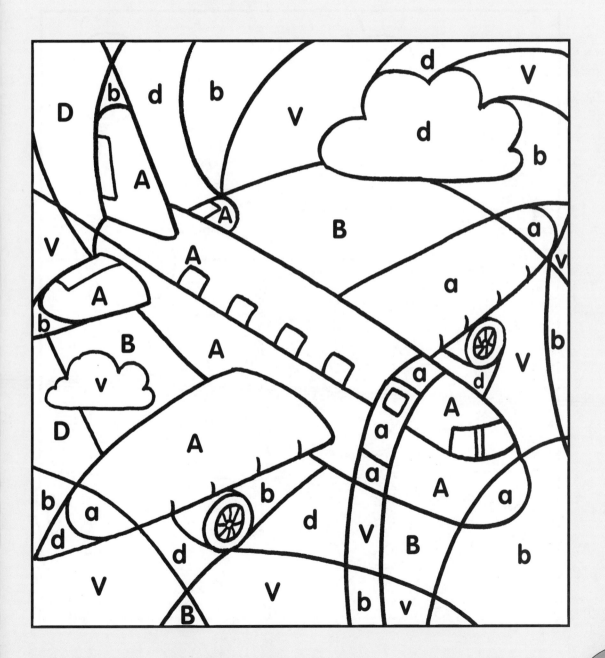

Busy Bears

Color the picture. Circle the things
that start with **Bb**.

Ben and the Boat

Help Ben find his boat.
Follow the path that shows **B** or **b**.

Cool Cat

Color the spaces that show **C** or **c**.

Car Trip

Color the picture. Circle the things that start with **Cc**.

The Dog's Dinner

Help the dog get to his dish. Follow the path that shows **D** or **d**.

D Is Delightful

Look at each picture. If it begins with the **Dd** sound, write **Dd** on the line below the picture.

Extra Big

Color the spaces that show **E** or **e**.

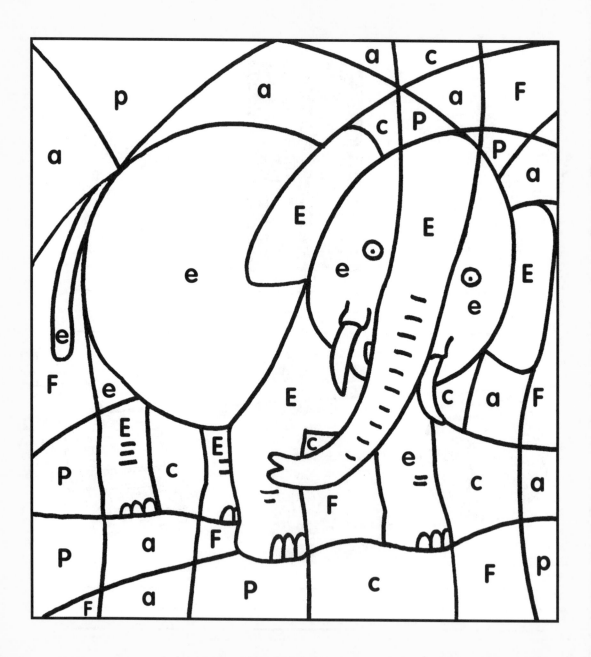

The Eagle's Eggs

Help the eagle get to her eggs. Follow the path that shows **E** or **e**.

F Is Fun

What animal has fun under the sea?
Color the spaces that show **F** or **f**.

A Few Flowers

Color the picture. Circle the things that start with **Ff**.

The Goose Is Loose

Help the goose get back to the garden. Follow the path that shows **G** or **g**.

A Great Gift

What did Gary get for his birthday? To find out, color
the spaces that show **G** or **g**.

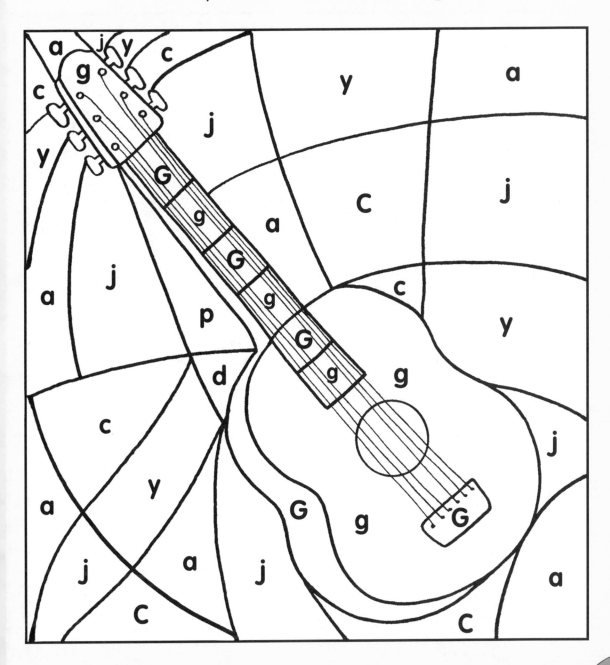

Hooray for H!

Color the picture. Circle the things that start with **Hh**.

Hungry Horse

Help the hungry horse get to the hay. Follow the path that shows **H** or **h**.

It's Icy

What kind of house is made of ice? To find out,
color the spaces that show **I** or **i**.

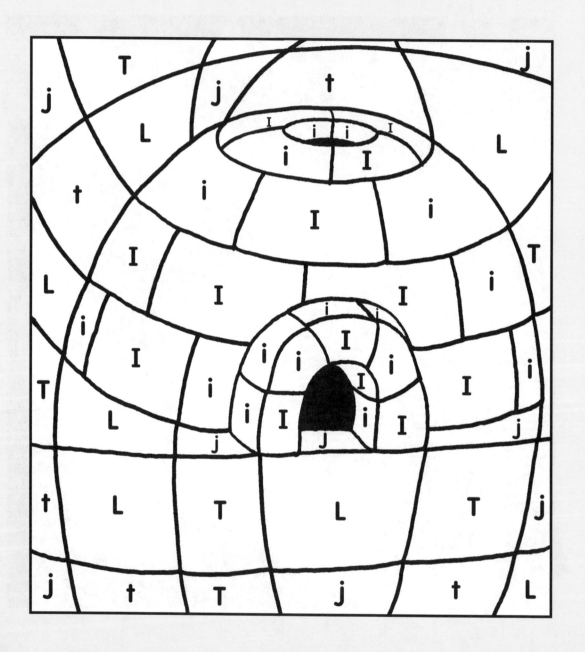

I Scream for Ice Cream

Help Isabel get to the ice cream store. Follow the path that shows **I** or **i**.

Jumping for J

Color the picture. Circle the things that start with **Jj**.

Jim and Jill Jog

Help Jim and Jill jog to the jungle gym.
Follow the path that shows **J** or **j**.

Up and Away

What can fly but has no wings? To find out, color all
the spaces that show **K** or **k**.

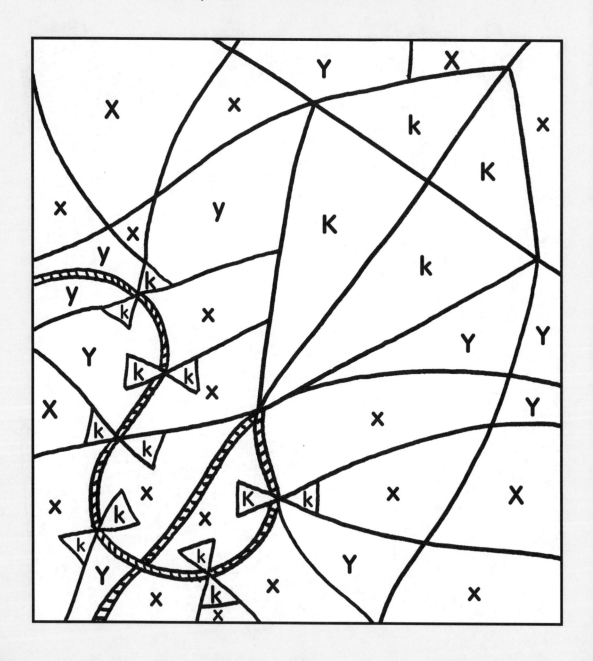

All Kinds of K Words

Look at each picture. If it begins with the **Kk** sound, write **Kk** on the line below the picture.

A Large Lad

Who is the king of the jungle? To find out, color all of the spaces that show **L** or **l**.

Lots of L Words

Color the picture. Circle the things that start with **Ll**.

Monkey Maze

Help the monkey find his mother. Follow the path that shows **M** or **m**.

Mr. Mouse

Is there a mouse in the house? To find out,
color all the spaces that show **M** or **m**.

N Is Nice

Look at each picture. If it begins with the **Nn** sound, write **Nn** on the line below the picture.

Oodles of Noodles

Nick loves noodles. Help Nick find his lunch.
Follow the path that shows **N** or **n**.

Whoooooo?

Who is hiding in the tree? To find out,
color all the spaces that show **O** or **o**.

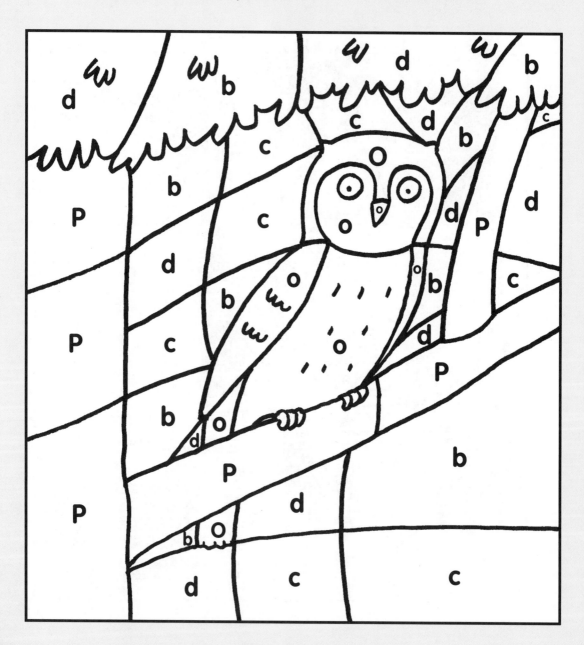

Oscar the Octopus

Help Oscar find his way back to the ocean.
Follow the path that shows **O** or **o**.

Playful Parade

Color the picture. Circle the animals
that begin with **Pp**.

Perfect P

What kind of "apple" does not grow on an apple tree?
To find out, color in the spaces that show **P** or **p**.

The Queen's Quilt

Look at the queen's quilt. Color the patches that show **Q** or **q**.

Quick, Quinn!

Help Quinn escape from the quicksand.
Follow the path that shows **Q** or **q**.

The Robot Is Ready

Color the spaces that show **R** or **r**.

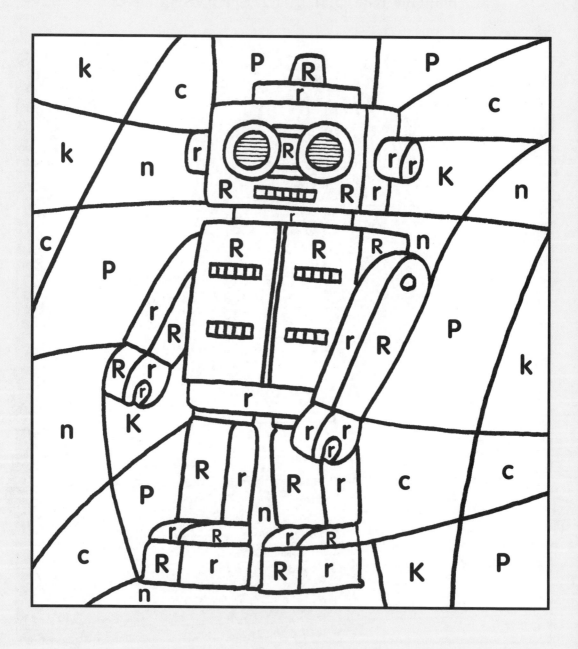

Rainy Day

Color the picture. Circle the things that begin with **Rr**.

S Is Super

Look at each picture. If it begins with the **Ss** sound, write **Ss** on the line below the picture.

Splash, Splash!

Color the picture. Circle the things that begin with **Ss**.

Tub Time

Color the picture. Circle the things that begin with **Tt**.

Tom's Toy Truck

Help Tom get his toy truck.
Follow the path that shows **T** or **t**.

Under an Umbrella

Color the spaces that show **U** or **u**.

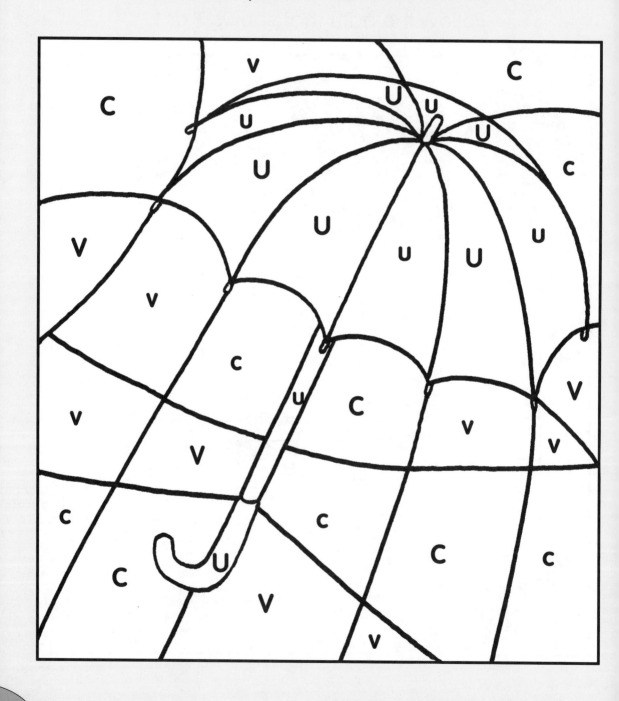

Ursula's Uncle

Help Ursula get to her uncle's house.
Follow the path that shows **U** or **u**.

A Valentine Surprise

Color the spaces that show **V** or **v**.

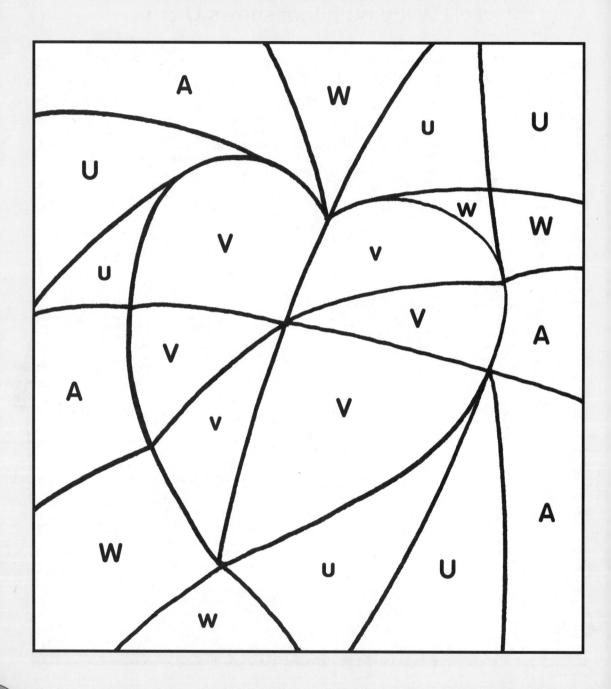

Violet's Violin

Help Violet get to her violin before the concert begins.
Follow the path that shows **V** or **v**.

W Is Wonderful

Look at each picture. If it begins with the **Ww** sound, write **Ww** on the line below the picture.

Winnie's Wedding

Help Winnie get to her wedding on time.
Follow the path that shows **W** or **w**.

Excellent X

Look at each picture. If it has the **Xx** sound,
write **Xx** on the line below the picture.

Max and the Box

Help Max get his things to the box. Follow the path that shows **X** or **x**.

Yell for Y

Look at each picture. If it begins with the **Yy** sound, write **Yy** on the line below the picture.

Yolanda's Yard

Help Yolanda get to her yard.

Follow the path that shows **Y** or **y**.

Z Is Zippy

Look at each picture. If it has the **Zz** sound,
write **Zz** on the line below the picture.

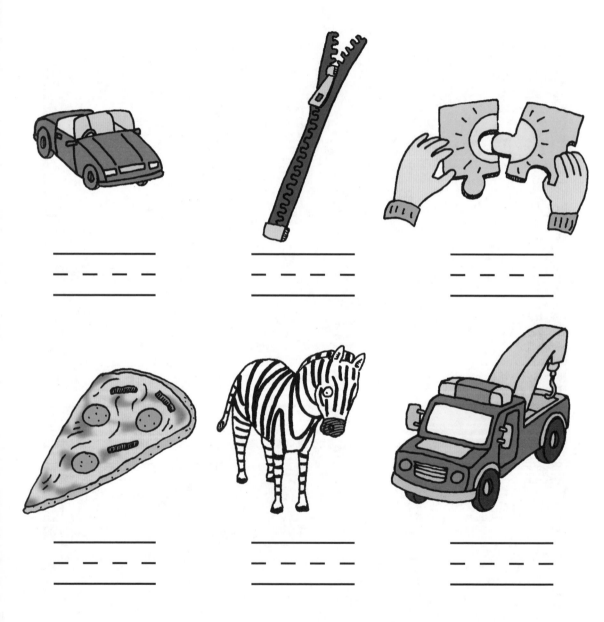

Zeke the Zebra

Help Zeke get back to the zoo.
Follow the path that shows **Z** or **z**.

Where Do You Live?

Connect the dots from **A** to **F**.
Color the picture.

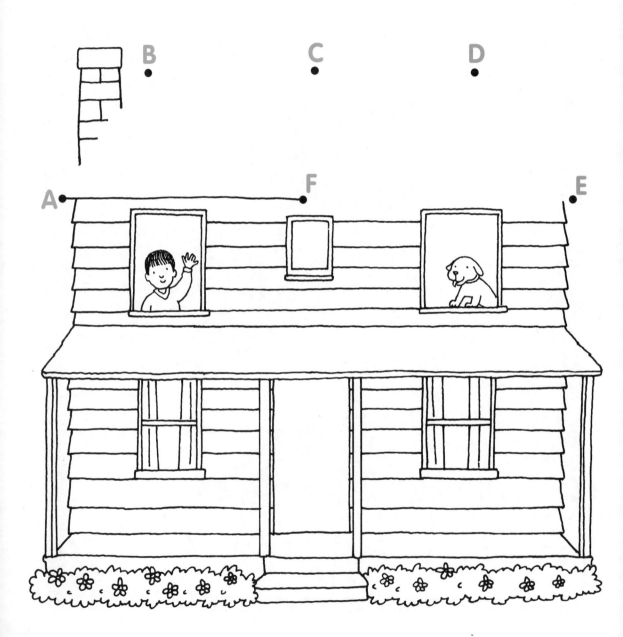

Going to School

Connect the dots from **G** to **L**.

Color the picture.

Where Do You Play?

Connect the dots from **M** to **R**.

Color the picture.

Where Do You Sleep?

Connect the dots from **S** to **Z**.

Color the picture.

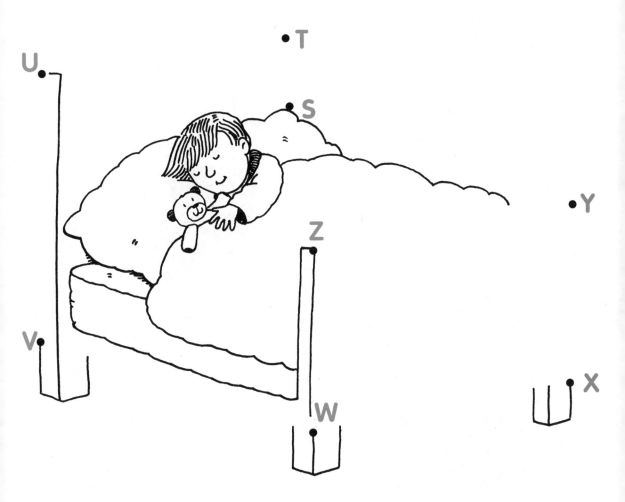

Make a Match

Draw a line between matching uppercase and lowercase letters.

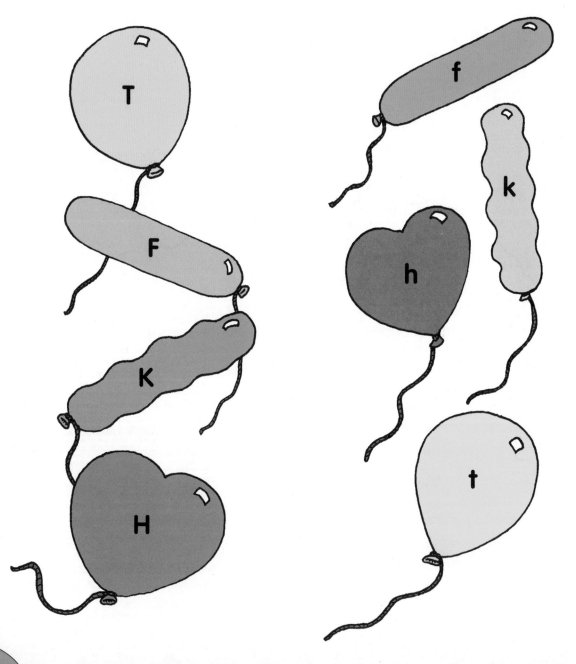

More Matching

Draw a line between matching uppercase
and lowercase letters.

Letter Match

Draw a line between matching uppercase and lowercase letters.

Big Fish, Small Fish

Draw a line between matching uppercase
and lowercase letters.

Great Job!

Give yourself an A+

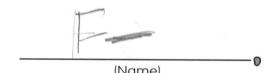

_____,
(Name)

now you know the alphabet!